John Dunlap Wells

The Last Week in the Life of Davis Johnson, Jr.

John Dunlap Wells

The Last Week in the Life of Davis Johnson, Jr.

ISBN/EAN: 9783337110147

Printed in Europe, USA, Canada, Australia, Japan

Cover: Foto ©ninafisch / pixelio.de

More available books at **www.hansebooks.com**

THE LAST WEEK

IN THE LIFE

OF

DAVIS JOHNSON, JR.

BY

J. D. WELLS,

PASTOR OF THE SOUTH THIRD STREET PRESBYTERIAN CHURCH,
WILLIAMSBURGH, L. I.

NEW YORK:
ROBERT CARTER & BROTHERS,
No. 530 BROADWAY.

1861.

"Oh, Sacred Providence, who from end to end,
    Strongly and sweetly movest! shall I write,
And not of Thee, through whom my fingers bend
    To hold my quill? shall they not do Thee right?"

CONTENTS.

CHAPTER I.

INTRODUCTORY.

"BE YE THEREFORE READY ALSO: FOR THE SON OF MAN
COMETH AT AN HOUR WHEN YE THINK NOT."　　JESUS.

"He was
A youth of noble form and feature,
A being sent to bless this world, and probe
To scoffers, that there is a God who rules
Above; for who but God could work thus nobly?"

I.

On Saturday, the 18th of July, 1857, Davis Johnson, Jr., received a mortal hurt while bathing in the East River, Williamsburgh, Long Island.

At the post-mortem examination, it was found, that the sixth cervical vertebra was broken into six pieces, and thrown out of place. There was consequently a compression of the spinal cord, and an entire paralysis of the nerves of motion and sensation, below the chest.

In this condition of body, and in the full possession of all his mental powers, he lived a whole week, expiring on Saturday, the 25th of July, just before night. He was not quite twenty years old.

The following pages are a simple record, chiefly from notes taken at the time, of his experience, the efforts made for his salvation, and the result, which, through the tender mercy of God, it is believed was secured, during that last week of his life.

And this record is now published, with the humble hope and prayer, that God may bless it to young men, and others into whose hands it shall fall.

CHAPTER II.

The Bath-House.

"ARE NOT TWO SPARROWS SOLD FOR A FARTHING? AND
ONE OF THEM SHALL NOT FALL ON THE GROUND WITHOUT
YOUR FATHER."   JESUS.

"Broken in pieces all asunder,
        Lord! hunt me not,
        A thing forgot;
    Once a poor creature, now a wonder,—
        A wonder, tortured in the space
    Betwixt this world and that of grace."

II.

DAVIS left the office of the "Atlantic Mutual Insurance Company," in Wall Street, New York, where he held a responsible position, a little earlier than usual, to enjoy the luxury of a bath. His parents, and a younger brother, boarded in Williamsburgh, L. I., while his boarding-house was in Brooklyn. For a reason which will be stated in the sequel, he was anxious to take his brother with him to a sanctuary in Brooklyn, where he had attended the Sabbath before. This reason revealed, I think, the beginning of a gracious work in his soul, before the awful week, during which it was destined to be developed and

2

matured for eternity. His plan, as stated by himself, was this :—to come over to Williamsburgh, enjoy the bath with his brother, and then take him to Brooklyn.

But God's plan was different.

The brothers entered the bath-house, then lying at the foot of South Eighth Street, Williamsburgh, and, in company with several other young men, indulged in the manly sport of swimming and diving. There was one part of the house, to which, on account of its elevation, bathers were sometimes tempted to climb, for the purpose of diving; but they were excluded from it, by printed regulations, because of the possible exposure of their persons.

To this place, Davis climbed; and when told by the attendant that he was doing wrong, he instantly plunged into the water, and this was his fatal plunge. He soon rose to the surface; but his head, and hands, and feet hung heavily down. At first, his brother, who was not in the bath at the moment, thought he was sporting, as he was perfectly at home in the water. Perceiving however, that he was hurt, he hastened to his assistance. On raising his face from the water, he was told that he must carry him out, for he could not help himself.

It is cause for wonder and gratitude, to this day, that the younger brother should have been able to carry Davis on his shoulder, through the water and up the steps of the bath-house, to the platform; and still more, that he should have done it without destroying the precious life which had received so fearful a blow. It was clear afterwards, that the slightest change in the relative position of the head and body, must have been attended with the risk of instant death. And it is a greater wonder than even this, that the younger brother and his associates, without knowing the extent of Davis's injuries, should have safely removed him, as he was, to a carriage, and so conveyed him to the boarding-house of his parents in Washington Place, a distance of several blocks, and then up the stone steps in front, and the long flight of stairs leading to the second floor of the house. There was no skillful surgeon to give directions and help, in this most delicate task; but surely the angels of God had him in charge, or he must have been killed.

It was a very merciful arrangement for the mother, that she was absent from the house, when her wounded boy was brought home to die. And on her return, shortly after, she was prepared for the tidings awaiting her, by the younger son, who considerately and tenderly met her at the door, and told her not to be alarmed, that Davis was hurt, but they hoped not seriously. And this was the impression of Davis himself. He was not overcome, therefore, when his mother, to whom he was bound by a filial love that I have never seen surpassed, came to his bed-side. His fine face was not marred, and there was no bruise on any part of his body. He said himself that he did not strike his head on the bottom of the bath; and this was manifestly the case, because there was not the slightest abrasion of the skin perceptible, and there was no pain. An intelligent physician expressed the opinion, that his forehead struck the water a little at one side, and when his head and body were not in a right line with each other. The consequence was, that his head was thrown violently back, and also to one side; and the cartilage uniting the bones not giving way, the sixth vertebra of the neck was literally pulled asunder and broken into six pieces. It was also twisted around, so that the spinous process was quite out of line with the spinous processes of the other vertebræ of the spinal column.

The pain that Davis felt was not great at first, and it was confined to one little spot in the neck. He could talk, and move his arms at will. His respiration was easy, and his heart beat with its usual force and regularity. And yet his body, below a line crossing the chest near the nipples, was dead; the process of digestion was permanently interrupted, and all sensation and power of motion were gone forever.

In this condition of body, and with no serious thoughts about his soul, he entered upon his last earthly Sabbath.

It is proper to add here, that to the last, Davis persisted in taking upon himself, all the blame of his fatal injury. More than once he exclaimed in my hearing: "I brought it all on myself." And this is now recorded, as a frank acknowledgment, alike honorable to him and due to the proprietors of the bath-house. He felt and said, that if he had obeyed the known laws of the place, he could not have been hurt.

CHAPTER III.

The Day of Preparation.

"As many as I love, I rebuke and chasten."
JESUS.

"Lead, Saviour, lead, amid the encircling gloom,
    Lead thou me on:
The night is dark, and I am far from home,
    Lead thou me on.
Keep thou my feet; I do not ask to see
The distant scene—one step, enough for me."

I I I.

THIS was a day of solemn preparation for the scenes that followed.

It is one of the precious truths of the Scriptures, that, " Like as a father pitieth his children, so the LORD pitieth them that fear him."—Ps. ciii., 13. We ought not to explain these words away. It is our duty, and privilege, to rise from our parental pity, of which we are so keenly sensible, to that of our Heavenly Father, of which we have need to assure ourselves.

The parents of Davis were not forgotten of God. They spent the day in ministering to his wants, and in yielding their hearts, hour after hour, more fully to the distressing conviction that he must die. He retained his consciousness throughout the day, while lying perfectly helpless. Indeed, his mind seemed to be active and clear, until he was struck with death.

You could puncture his cold flesh with a pin, at any point below the line of sensibility, across his chest, without his knowledge; but the instant you crossed that invisible, mysterious line, he would cry out with pain. His arms and fingers obeyed the dictates of his will, and retained their sensibility, though not wholly unimpaired, for at times they tingled as if "asleep;" and again they were acutely sensitive, so that he could not bear to have them touched. This morbid sensibility was particularly distressing in the wrists, and palms of the hands. His head was, of course, immovable, because of the fracture of the neck;

but, his vocal powers, and the muscles of his face, were as true to his volitions as ever. He could, therefore, talk freely with physicians and friends, about his changing sensations, and the thoughts and emotions of his soul.

Recourse was had, during the day, to various means, and among them, electricity, with the hope of restoring the lost powers of sensation and motion, to his body and legs, but without effect.

His removal, from the bed to a cot, cost him indescribable suffering, and confirmed the judgment of the physicians, that his injury must soon prove fatal; and they thought it clearly their duty, to reveal their fears, and the ground of them, to the distressed parents. This they did; but it is easy to understand how, against hope, they still clung to hope; for, to the eye,

3

there was no wound upon the person of the sufferer. He looked the very picture of health. I had not seen him, indeed, up to this point; but the same healthful appearance of his face and body continued, till the powers of life were exhausted. It was only at intervals, and when he was greatly prostrated, that we could persuade ourselves of the approach of death.

Had he been a youth of feeble constitution, he must have sunk much sooner; but he had the vigour and muscular development, of a man several years his senior. This proved an unspeakable mercy to him, in the end, though it prolonged and greatly aggravated his sufferings. As a lost sinner, on the borders of eternity, he needed all his strength, physical and mental; and that this was continued, until, through grace, he was enabled to lay hold on eternal life, was the occasion, at last, of many thanksgivings unto God.

But he had no serious apprehensions of danger, and no thought of pleading for mercy, up to the close of the Sabbath.

CHAPTER IV.

The Awakening.

"AND WHEN HE IS COME, HE WILL REPROVE THE WORLD
OF SIN, AND OF RIGHTEOUSNESS, AND OF JUDGMENT."

JESUS.

———————

"The Spirit, like some heabenly wind,
  Blows on the sons of flesh;
New models all the carnal mind,
  And forms the man afresh."

IV.

THIS was the first day, marked by deep spiritual concern on the part of Davis, and by the earnest efforts of Christian friends, for his salvation.

As he awoke about 3 o'clock in the morning, his mother, watching beside him, said :

"You are very ill, my son!"

"Not very," he answered cheerfully.

"But you are very ill, Davis. Don't you feel that you are ?"

"No! I am not much hurt; I shall be out in a few days."

If his mother had cared only for his present comfort, she would have left him under the illusion that his injury was slight. This, alas! is the frequent treatment of the sick; they are robbed of the golden hours that remain to them of life, lest the use of those hours in preparing for death, should hurry their passage to the grave.

Mrs. Johnson had reason to believe that her son was unreconciled to God; she thought of his soul, and of the infinite value of even moments of time, to one in his circumstances; and again, with a bleeding heart, she pressed upon him the fact of his extreme danger.

"You will not be well in a few days, and you may never recover."

He asked with kindling emotion, "Why do you say so, mother?"

"Because it is the opinion of your physicians."

This was a moment of bitter anguish to both mother and child; and it was followed by many hours of greater anguish; but how salutary and necessary!

His next words were these, "I can't die." With a fearful emphasis breathed into the utterance, he exclaimed more than once, "*I* CAN'T die!" "I *can't* DIE!"

"Can't you pray, my son?"

"Pray!" said he; "God knows I wouldn't have been praying, if I hadn't been hurt. I can't pray. Do pray for me. *Now* pray for me."

His mother knelt by his cot, and besought the Lord to have mercy on her dying son; she also begged him to join her in praying for himself, which he tried to do.

After this, the agitation of his mind was somewhat calmed, and when he was asked if he would like to see me, he answered quickly: "Oh yes! do send for him as soon as you can in the morning."

Thus far in the narrative I have relied

upon the vivid recollections of Mrs. Johnson, for what has been said of the state of Davis's mind.

Beyond this point, my dependence is almost exclusively upon notes taken by myself, after each interview.

And I may as well say here, and once for all, that having come to the conclusion, after much reflection, that I ought to publish this account of Mr. Johnson's awakening and conversion to God, as I believe it was, I shall not spoil the narrative by constant apologies for speaking so much in the first person. I am obliged to speak in this way, or not at all. It is a very humble agency any one has, in winning a soul to Christ. The new creation of the sinner, and his eternal union to the person of the Redeemer, can be effected only by the Holy Spirit: and it is my earnest desire to bring this young man before my readers as in the hands of the Spirit of God, and passing from stage to stage of his short and painful course, drawn irresistibly forward, by the attractions revealed to him in the cross and the Person of Christ. Succeeding in this, I shall be satisfied, and cherish the hope that some who read these pages, will bless God forever, that they were written.

I proceed with the narrative.

Early in the morning of this day, I was requested by Mr. Davis Johnson, who with his wife, is a member of my Church, to visit his son. I had heard nothing of his injury. As we walked together towards his boarding-house, he told me the facts, in brief, of the distressing accident; also that a council of physicians had expressed the opinion that Davis could not possibly recover, and that he would not probably live more than three or four days. A few words were added about the painful agitation of his mind.

I need not say that the responsibility of becoming his spiritual guide in these distressing circumstances, weighed heavily upon me. I told the father that I could not think of assuming it, without being faithful to his son from the first; that I must tell him of his sins with very great plainness, and not leave him in ignorance of the opinion expressed by the physicians, that he must soon die.

On coming to his cot, therefore, I at once threw myself on the judgment of his physicians, and begged him to regard himself, as near the eternal world.

He was silent and intensely earnest, in his attention to what I said.

I then asked him as tenderly as possible, if he thought himself ready to stand before God, and give account of his life? His answer was a loud wail that pierced my heart like a knife. He cried out in agony—

he said that he could not die—he had broken God's commandments, and must go to hell.

His mind sprang to this conclusion with awful precision and swiftness, and his lips uttered it without the slightest hesitation.

Moreover, he justified God, saying then and often afterwards, that it was right and necessary that he should perish, for he would not mind God, and was not prepared to be happy in heaven.

Distressing as it was to witness his anguish, I was constrained to believe that he was even then, the subject of a true awakening by the Holy Ghost, and that He who had begun, would complete His own gracious and wonderful work. Pointing him to Christ the compassionate, almighty, and accessible Saviour, to whom the Holy Spirit then convincing him of sin, was waiting to lead him, and praying with him, I left, promising to call again in the afternoon.

As it is my purpose to make known the means used for securing the salvation of this young man, I attach great importance to the following statement. Whatever may be thought of it by the world, I am persuaded that the Christian reader will understand and appreciate it.

The Church of which I am pastor, was enjoying at the time of Davis's injury, the reviving presence of the Holy Spirit. The Sabbath before the Monday on which I first visited him, was one of unusual solemnity and interest, in our sanctuary. We were occupied all day, in contemplating our royal priesthood in Christ, and with special reference to the duty, and power, of intercession for others.

Accordingly, when I left Davis, I went immediately to some of my beloved people, who were prevalent in prayer, with the earnest request that they would take his

soul upon their souls, and plead for him.
And as I met others through the day, I
suggested that the Providence of our Lord,
was conspiring with his word and the Holy
Spirit, to teach us the efficacy of inter-
cessory prayer, and that we must not rest
while the sufferer lived. From that time,
till he slept in Jesus, "prayer was made,
without ceasing, of the Church unto God
for him," and it was not made in vain.

Calling in the afternoon, according to
promise, I found that Dr. Mott, of New
York, was with him, trying to reduce the
dislocation of the neck. This, of course,
precluded my seeing him, and led me to
adopt the plan of writing letters, to be read
in my absence, and as his strength would
permit. I felt that he needed instruction
out of the Scriptures, and that just as fast
and long as he could receive the truth, it
should be freely communicated to him, as

the instrument, in the hands of the Holy Spirit, not only of his regeneration and union to Christ, but also of his sanctification and comfort. And I believe now that these letters were a blessing to him.

My first letter was accompanied by the following note to his parents, which is published, with their consent, because it expresses clearly the conviction of my mind, that Christian parents should coöperate fully with ministers in giving their dying children plain instruction from the Bible, though it may pain them to do so.

"July 20, 1857.

"My dear Mr. and Mrs. Johnson:

"My heart bleeds for you, and pours out prayer in your behalf. May God support you, and make you faithful to your dear, dying son.

"I need not pray you not to heal slightly the hurt of his poor soul. You would not for worlds do this, and I would not for the treasure of the universe.

"I have written a letter which I hope you will first read by yourselves, and then may you have strength to read it to your son. Do not keep back the truth of God from him. He will bless you eternally for faithful instruction, and warning, and entreaty, and for fervent, believing prayer.

"Do not divert his mind from his sins. It is the Holy Spirit, I trust, who quickens his conscience. He must see, and feel, and deplore his sins. Tell him this, and when his soul is in agony, point him to Christ, and lead him to Christ. Take his soul upon your souls, and go before him to Jesus, in faith and prayer; and though you bury your dear boy, you shall find him in the resurrection.

"Again I beseech you not to withhold from him the truth that tells him of his sins. I will call in the morning, if spared, and will continue to write the truths that I hope and pray God may bless to your dying son. Affectionately, your pastor,

"J. D. WELLS."

In printing this note, it is hardly necessary to say, that the parents of Davis most earnestly and gratefully seconded all that was done to lead him to Christ; while they also went before all others, in personal desires and efforts for his salvation.

The first letter to him was as follows:

"PARSONAGE, July 20, 1857.

"MY DEAR MR. JOHNSON:

"I called this afternoon, but could not see you, without interrupting those who were trying to relieve your wounded body.

"May I take this way of addressing you? Most truly can I say, that you have lain upon my heart, from the time that I first

4*

heard of your injury. Never have I felt a greater and more painful responsibility thrown upon me, than now. You would justly despise me for ever, if I should keep back any of those great and precious truths, by which, through God's blessing, you may be saved from eternal death, though at the last hour of your earthly life. I think I hear you say to parents, minister, and friends: 'Do not trifle with me. Tell me the truth, and tell it plainly, while God gives me strength to hear it; and when I cannot speak to you any more, still speak to me the words of eternal life, and pray for me.' We will do this, my dear young friend.

"Let me beg you, first of all, to believe that your injury is so serious, that all the ground of hope you can have of living more than a few days, is as nothing. I write this with deepest grief; but you do not wish to be deceived.

"I pray you next to believe, that though your sins be as scarlet and crimson in the sight of the Holy God, to whom your spirit will soon return, there is a way made very plain in the Bible, in which you may even now be freely pardoned and made holy; for without holiness no man shall see the Lord.

"And now do not refuse to believe exactly what God says of your sinfulness. He knows your heart, and He tells you what is in your heart. He lays it bare. The Holy Spirit comes as Jesus said He would, to 'reprove the world of sin, and of righteousness, and of judgment.' You know, dear sir, that you have broken God's law. It is holy, just, and good. But you have not loved it, and you have not kept it. 'The carnal mind is enmity against God; for, it is not subject to the law of God, neither indeed can be.' And thus you are lost. You are under the curse of God's

law, and near eternity.   But, oh, my dying
and lost friend, God Himself offers to save
you.   He tells you of His dear Son.   He
invites, and commands, and entreats you to
look and come to Jesus.

"'Behold the Lamb of God that taketh
away the sin of the world.   His blood
cleanseth us from all sin.   He is able to
save to the uttermost all that come unto
God by Him.   Believe on the Lord Jesus
Christ, and thou shalt be saved.   Repent
and believe the Gospel.'

"Affectionately yours,

"J. D. WELLS."

CHAPTER V.

Conviction Prolonged.

"FOR I WAS ALIVE WITHOUT THE LAW ONCE: BUT WHEN THE COMMANDMENT CAME, SIN REVIVED AND I DIED."

PAUL.

"Poor, lost, benighted soul, art thou
 Willing to find salvation now?—
 There yet is hope,—hear mercy's call,—
 Truth, life, light, way, in Christ is all!
  Haste to HIM, haste!"

V.

My interview with Davis this morning was very affecting. At his request, his younger brother, and he alone, remained in the room with us. The reason for this he gave, revealing not only a true fraternal devotion, but, I had almost said, a Christian love, which grew stronger and stronger to the last. He expressed the hope that his brother might be profited by the conversation. He wished him to hear what he was about to say with eternity in view, and also what I might say, as a Christian minister, in the name of Christ.

Having thus arranged everything for our interview, he. proceeded, without the least

hesitation, and with great solemnity, to say
to me, as if no one else had been present,
"I know that I must die very soon, and
that I am lost; I am not fit to die; I cannot
go to heaven; I must go to hell. It is
right that I should; I deserve to perish;
I would not mind God; I would not be
good; I knew what God said I must do,
but I would not do it; I did not like to."

In very simple words like these, he uttered again and again his own condemnation;
while, in terms as clear and strong as could
be used, he justified God. This was a
striking and hopeful feature of his experience from the first; and it was the
more impressive, because, not being accustomed to express himself on such subjects,
there was nothing technical or set in his
phrases. I could not resist the conviction,
that the Holy Spirit was leading him safely
into the truth; though it was most distress-

ing to witness his anguish, and to hear the words in which he poured out his complaint; nor was it possible to give him relief. God's time had not yet come for revealing the Saviour to him. Full and free salvation was offered him in the name of Christ. I told him the story of the cross as simply and tenderly as I could; he was reminded of the personal glory of the living and accessible Redeemer, of His offices, His work, and His death; the very words of Jesus and His inspired servants, were repeated and explained, to allure and help him; and then fervent intercession was made for him. But the sentence of his righteous condemnation, was written before the eye of his consciousness too plainly to be overlooked; the wrath of God was revealed from heaven against him. Though young, he was made to feel that he had treasured up wrath against the day of wrath. I know of no scriptural terms that are too strong to express his conviction of personal guilt and vileness, and helpless exposure to punishment, as a sinner. The commandment, seen as he had never seen it before, to be holy, just, and good—though very imperfectly known yet, in its spirituality and breadth, as the experience of another day will show— was in the hands of the Holy Spirit to slay him. He was killed, and I could not make him live and rejoice before God, as a renewed and pardoned sinner.

He expressed the opinion, without reserve, that God could not possibly receive him as a child, and pass by his transgressions. He must undo his wrong, and lead a different life. And then, remembering that his days were numbered, he exclaimed, "Oh, if I could live eight or ten years, and show God that I would be good, I might be saved, but now I must die."

"Davis," I said, "if you could live a thousand years, you must be saved by coming to Christ as you are, and resting upon Him. All that you can do is utterly worthless to commend you to God. You must count your very righteousnesses as filthy rags, and, casting all away, accept of the perfect righteousness of God's dear Son, as a free gift to you personally. Do not yield to the dreadful thought that you must perish, because you have not years of life in prospect, when Jesus says, 'I am the resurrection and the life; he that believeth in me, though he were dead, yet shall he live: and whosoever liveth and believeth in me shall never die.' You know that His blood cleanseth us from all sin."

Still he did not, and could not consciously come to Christ. The perfect freeness of salvation, the accessibility of Jesus, the possibility of his having a full and eternal

pardon on account of the Saviour's sacrificial death, and merely for the taking, were
great mysteries, above his comprehension.
His eyes were holden that he could not see.
It pleased God to leave him a little longer
under the guilt of his sins, before shining
into his mind to give him the light of the
knowledge of the glory of God, in the face
of Jesus Christ.   And painful as it was, I
think his experience was most salutary, at
this time.   He learned, so as never to forget or doubt the great truth, that no man
can come to Christ, except he be drawn by
the Father; and that we can so discern the
glory of Jesus as to call him Lord, only by
the Holy Ghost.   It was truly refreshing,
after Jesus Christ was revealed to him, and
in him, to hear his unreserved and unquali-
fied ascription of all the praise to God.   He
could not withhold the ascription, because
he had effectually learned his helplessness.

After the interview of the morning, I remained to witness the examination of Davis's neck, by eminent surgeons of New York and Brooklyn. And I feel it to be at once a duty and pleasure, to state here, that Dr. T. L. Mason, of Brooklyn, who had the case in charge, manifested to the last, the most tender concern for the salvation of his patient. Believing his injury to be fatal, he deeply felt, as a Christian man, that everything should be made subordinate to his reconciliation with God. And he acted accordingly, sharing fully in the great joy of many hearts, when the salvation of God came, as we all believed, to the sufferer. He has never known, perhaps, how his Christian consideration comforted the family and friends of Davis, and drew forth prayers and thanksgivings on his account.

The examination had at this time revealed the fact, that the sixth cervical ver-

tebra was drawn forward and sideways out
of its place, but not the fact afterwards
learned, that it was broken into several
pieces. And as this latter fact was not
known, the thought was entertained of an
operation, having for its object the restora-
tion of the bone to its true place in the
spinal column.

It was distressing to leave Davis, so near
the eternal world, writhing under the strong
conviction of his exposure to God's just
wrath, and unable to see the way of life.
But there was no alternative. We may not
dictate to God, as to the fact, the time, or
any of the circumstances of a sinner's conversion. We can instruct the sinner, and
plead with him to be reconciled to God.
We may send up our petition to the throne
of the heavenly grace, putting it into the
hands of our Great High Priest, who ever
liveth to make intercession for us. But

what then? We may not clamour to be heard. We must not abuse the privilege of holy importunity. We are to wait on God, and wait for God. And many suppliants did this in behalf of Davis. His case excited extraordinary interest, and for the simple reason that, in every respect, it was an extraordinary case. He was the subject of special prayer that evening, and afterwards, in at least two sanctuaries; while his name was mentioned at many domestic and private altars.

The Rev. E. L. Janes, at that time pastor of the South Fifth Street M. E. Church, Williamsburgh, was a friend of the family, and manifested a very tender and intelligent interest in the welfare of Davis; in his church, therefore, prayer was offered.

And as for my own Church—our usual lecture was omitted, that we might fully consider the condition of the sufferer, and bring his case before God in prayer.

I told the people all that the physicians had then discovered and made known, as to his physical condition; of the probability that the proposed operation to reduce the dislocation of the neck, would result in instant death; and that for this reason the operation would be postponed till the latest possible moment, in the hope that he might be prepared for his change.

I told them also, particularly, of the deep and distressing convictions under which I left him in the morning. And then we tried to reflect upon the relations of an unpardoned soul to God, to all the provisions of grace revealed in the Scriptures, and to eternity. It was a night to be remembered. Our hearts were still under the influence of the great truths relating to our royal priesthood, that had been considered on the Sabbath; and the Holy Ghost, the Paraclete, was with us. Seldom is a company of supplicants placed in circumstances to see so vividly, that an immortal soul, trembling on the verge of the eternal world, without hope, must be rescued by their faith or lost forever; and most tender, fervent, and reverential intercessions went up to God from many hearts.

Dr. Duff, years ago, wrote of the effect produced in Calcutta on large numbers of the Hindoo young men, by the instructions of the missionaries. They were brought, in many instances, apparently to the verge of the kingdom of heaven, but there they stopped. Across the invisible line that divides that kingdom from the world, no demonstrations of science subverting their old superstitions, and no persuasions of love, could move them. Till God interposed in the sovereignty and might of His wondrous grace, they were lost, though rationally convinced of the truth of Christianity.

We deeply felt that, till God interposed to draw Davis to Christ by His word and Spirit, he was lost.

We can never know in this world, what connection the intercessions of that night, and the innumerable prayers of God's people in the closet, the family, and the sanctuary, had with the result soon to be mentioned. But I should think myself guilty of a sinful omission, if I did not give them a very prominent place among the divinely appointed and honoured means of his salvation.

And I venture to close the records of this day with a few inquiries that often press themselves upon my own heart for solution.

Why should we not feel as intense a desire for the salvation of every unpardoned sinner, to whom we have access, as for one in the appalling circumstances of Davis?

The perils of the soul are always great beyond conception, till refuge is found in the living Redeemer. How can we endure to see the destruction of our kindred?

How can we rest, while scores of our friends and neighbours, living in pleasures, are dead, according to the divine and published judgment?   .

Where are the bowels of our compassion for the whole world lying in wickedness?

The wail of a single dying sinner, distinctly heard, drives sleep from our eyes, and draws us together as earnest suppliants around the mercy-seat; but we have only to listen, and we shall hear the groans of thousands dying in their sins, shrinking back from the grave, not only with an instinctive horror, but with dark and reasonable forebodings of the eternal consequences of leaving this world as they are. Why are we not in sympathy with Jesus, who, giving us life in His blood, and in eternal connexion with His Person, by the indwelling of the Holy Ghost, asks and expects us to come to His help for the saving of the world? I pray that God may make any impressions the reader has received, in looking upon the dying youth of whom I am writing, minister to a permanent and ever-increasing desire for the salvation of souls.

The letter that follows was the second left with the parents of Davis, to be read to him in my absence:

"TUESDAY MORNING, July 21, 1857.

"MY DEAR MR. JOHNSON:

"You are still spared, in the great mercy of God, and can cry unto Him to save you. If He had wished your destruction, how easily could He have taken away your reason and consciousness! Be persuaded to believe that He now waits to be gracious; and do not delay a moment longer to flee for refuge, to lay hold upon the hope set before you in the gospel.

"Let me urge you, first, to turn away from father, mother, ministers, and friends; for they cannot give relief to your poor body; much less can they save your soul and body from the curse, the power, and the vileness of sin. Your only help is in the very God whose law you have broken, and whose dear Son you have refused to believe and obey.

"And I beg you next, not to form your opinion of your character from the judgment of men, and the commendations of friends who tenderly love you; but from the true, and searching, and blessed word of God. Dismiss the thought from your mind, that you are fit to appear with joy and safety before God. Remember, I entreat you, that though you had been kept from all immoralities, from profaneness, sabbath-breaking, and other open transgressions, you have not been kept from the sin of rejecting the Son of God as your Saviour. This is the great sin of men, all unbelieving men, in a Christian land. So the Saviour Himself teaches.

"Remember, further, my dear sir, that you must be convinced of sin, your own sin; that you are such a sinner as God says you are; that your sins make you vile in the sight of God; that they justly expose you to the displeasure of God; and that you are helpless, lying before God, at His mercy.

"These are great and distressing truths, but they are salutary; and may our gracious God bless them to you. And now, will you pray for the Holy Spirit to give you this conviction? It is His work; and you must, you will, look to Him. Let your dying breath be spent in pleading for the Holy Spirit. He will not only convince you of sin, but effectually change your heart, and lead you to Christ. *You must be born again.* You must receive and rest upon Jesus Christ as your own Saviour. My heart is grieved for you, that you have delayed this momentous work till now; but do not delay another moment. Though your sins be as scarlet, and your time so short, Jesus can and will save you, if you will cast yourself upon Him alone for salvation. Once more I beseech you to do this, and I pray that you may be persuaded and enabled to do it.

"Sincerely your friend,

"J. D. WELLS."

There is one point in this letter, on which I am constrained to remark, in a sentence or two. Possibly some awakened sinner reading it, may have his mind confused, as to the precise thing he must do to be saved.

"Let your dying breath," I wrote to Davis, "be spent in pleading for the Holy Spirit." Taken in their connexion, especially in connexion with the repeated oral instructions he received, to look to Jesus, to come to Jesus, and to believe on the Lord Jesus Christ, I do not think there was any danger that these words would divert his attention from Christ. And now, what the reader must do to be saved, is to believe on the Lord Jesus Christ. Apply to Him at once, and, of course, just as you are. You need a broken heart, and the pardon of your sins; but He is exalted a Prince and a Saviour, to give repentance to Israel, and forgiveness of sins. Remember that He baptizeth with the Holy Ghost, and that it is right to ask Him for this baptism. Your asking for it is an application, a coming to Him. Rest upon Him, then. It is the Living Person you want. Seek Him, rather than salvation, and you will have salvation, in Him, "Who of God is made unto us wisdom, and righteousness, and sanctification, and redemption; that, according as it is written, He that glorieth, let him glory in the Lord."

6*

CHAPTER VI.

A Fatal Delusion.—The Crisis.

"Insomuch that, if it were possible, they shall de·
ceive the very elect."   JESUS.

"Lord Jesu, thou didst bow
Thy dying head upon the tree:
Oh, be not now
More dead to me!
Lord, hear! Shall He that made the ear not hear?"

VI.

At the morning visit I found Davis not perceptibly weaker in body than yesterday. He was still suffering under the crushing weight of his unpardoned sins. He could not find the way of life. All the energies of his soul seemed to be expended on the momentous inquiry, "What must I do to be saved?"

He had been thinking deeply on the subject, and startled me at last by saying with perfect frankness :

"I do not see that God can receive me, till after I have suffered in hell."

This sentence alone, of all that Davis uttered during that remarkable week, shocked and alarmed me. It showed that he was not yet really slain by the law of God, and that he knew but little of its holiness, spirituality, breadth, and pure justice. It was a revelation of very imperfect views of the malignity and vileness of his sins, and of his own ill desert on account of them. It implied a rejection of the plainest truths of the Scripture, as to the eternity of future punishments. And then it showed that notwithstanding his bitter anguish of soul, and his apparently sincere approval of God's condemning sentence under which he lay, he was still so blind as utterly to overlook the Person and the atonement of the Lord Jesus Christ, as his only hope.

Most earnestly did I labour to show him that he was hiding in a refuge of lies; that his doom was indeed sealed forever, if, with the Bible in his hands, and the opportunity of knowing the truth as it is in Jesus, he should die clinging to the wretched hope he had just expressed. It was shown to be a false hope. I did not know at the time its origin in his heart; it seemed to me like a strong delusion—a fiery dart injected into his mind—to destroy him at the last moment.

I have since learned that some of his associates were Universalists and Restorationists. He had heard their views thrown out in the freedom of debate, and though he did not consciously embrace them, they left their deadly impress on his heart. And how congenial to the human heart are such views! It is a marvellous demonstration of the power of truth, the supremacy of conscience, and the grace of Jesus, that there are no more Universalists and Restorationists in Christendom. But how should our sons and daughters be grounded in the truth, before they are, exposed in society,

4*

to the remotest suggestions of this most insidious and dangerous of all heresies!

In Davis's mind there was a distinct, though not hitherto influential impression, that sinners might possibly be saved after a period of suffering—longer or shorter, according to their deserts—in hell. Driven by the truth and Spirit of God to the borders of despair, and ready to catch at any straw of hope, rather than fall, as he was, into the arms of Christ, he caught at this straw. "The heart," I believe, "is deceitful above all things and desperately wicked." I believe also in the personal agency of Satan, and that he employed all his wiles and power at this fearful crisis, to deceive and so destroy one whom God loved; but he was foiled, and his power was broken by a stronger than he. To our conquering LORD be all the glory.

The mind of Davis had great vigour, and

he was remarkably candid and open to conviction; moreover he was intensely anxious to know the truth. When, therefore, it was spoken to him with authority and love, in the name of Christ, his whole nature bowed before it, as a tree is moved by the wind of heaven. And though it cost him the pang of renouncing all the hope he had—a hope that was indeed a lie and would soon have made him ashamed—he was enabled to do it.

He was in total darkness, struggling with the waves of despair and death. For the moment his hand had found what seemed to support him, and though it was piercing him through with many sorrows, he could not leave it. But when he heard the voice of the Beloved, louder than the noise of many waters, saying to him tenderly yet firmly: "Look unto me and be saved;" "Come unto me;" he did leave it. He bravely let go his hold, to struggle on toward Jesus, with only His voice to guide him through the billows and the darkness. When I parted with him after prayer, his soul was searching as never before, for Christ, the only name under heaven, given among men, whereby we must be saved.

The time of his deliverance was at hand.

The following letter, the last that I had occasion to write, was left with his mother, and read to him :

"PARSONAGE, WEDNESDAY MORNING, July 22, 1857.

"DEAR MR. JOHNSON :"

"THE Lord Jesus is able to save to the uttermost all that come unto God by Him. He is God's own and only Son; and He became flesh and dwelt among men full of grace and truth. But this is not all the wonder of his condescension; He died upon the cross. He loved us and gave Himself for us. He was wounded for our transgressions. He was bruised for our iniquities, and the chastisement of our peace was upon Him. It pleased God to put Him to shame, and to make Him to be sin for us, that we might be made the righteousness of God in Him. He was delivered for our offences, and was raised again for our justification. And now He is exalted at the right hand of God, a Prince and a Saviour to give repentance to Israel and forgiveness of sins, and His blood cleanseth us from all sin.

"This is good tidings of great joy for you; you may be saved from all the consequences and vileness of your sins, by faith in Jesus Christ. The plan is God's; the offer of eternal life is made by God Himself, who knows all your sins; and will you not believe that He is willing to save you? Do you ask : 'What must I do to be saved?' I answer in the words of inspiration, ' Believe on the Lord Jesus Christ and thou shalt be saved,' Acts xvi. 31. Here, my dear friend,

is God in your own nature, who has died on
purpose to save sinners. He can save you;
and if you will just believe on Him, cast
yourself upon Him, quietly rest upon Him,
you shall be saved. Do not delay, and
do not doubt. You have not to earn your
salvation; you cannot; no one can or ever
did. We are all to be saved in the same way,
by accepting Jesus Christ as our Saviour,
and giving ourselves up to Him, to change
our hearts; to make us truly penitent for
sin; to secure the pardon of all our sins;
to make us holy; to support us in death;
to receive our souls and present them to His
Father in heaven; to raise us from the
dead; and to acquit us at the judgment.

"Do not wait to be any better, before
hoping that God will accept you for Jesus's
sake. He will accept you only as a sinner.
'They that be whole need not a physician,
but they that are sick.' Jesus said that.

And now, it is the poor sinner that worketh not, but believeth on Him that justifieth the ungodly, that is accounted righteous and shall be saved.'—Romans iv., 5.

"With much sympathy and prayer,
"Your friend,
"J. D. WELLS."

Here, perhaps, better than elsewhere, I may state, that an extraordinary interest was shown by many persons in the welfare of young Mr. Johnson.

He received this day an excellent letter from a Christian gentleman, long his friend, urging him to apply to Christ for eternal life, and assuring him of earnest prayer in his behalf.

But the most affecting tribute to his worth, outside of his own family, was that which came from the officers, and many of the clerks, of the "Atlantic Mutual Insurance Company." Day and night they were with him. To one of the Vice-Presidents he was dear as a son; and he, with some of his associates, manifested an interest in his recovery, or his preparation for death, rarely witnessed. One cannot but ask why it is so rare? And why does it not reveal itself before death is at hand to dissolve their relations forever? Surely the officers of our Insurance Companies, Banks, and other corporate bodies, together with Merchants and Masters of all grades, are solemnly bound to watch for the souls of their young men, as they that must give account.

Davis had the confidence and love of his employers. Apt to learn, and reliable, he was rapidly advanced to a place of great responsibility, performing duties never before intrusted, in that company, to one so young.

He had his faults; but when told of them

in the spirit of kindness, he frankly owned the truth, and promised not to repeat them. Nor was he known to break his word. The law of truth was in his lips.

When he was stricken down, therefore, manly tears were shed for him, and prayers were breathed for his salvation, by Christian gentlemen, who had hitherto known little more of him, than that he was doing excellent service for them. And when it was known that, after his fearful anguish of spirit, he was rejoicing in hope of the glory of God, there was great joy among them, as well as in many other circles on earth, and in the presence of the angels of God in heaven.

CHAPTER VII.

Salvation.

"AND THIS IS THE WILL OF HIM THAT SENT ME, THAT EVERY ONE WHICH SEETH THE SON, AND BELIEVETH ON HIM, MAY HAVE EVERLASTING LIFE; AND I WILL RAISE HIM UP AT THE LAST DAY." JESUS.

———————

"Oh, that I might some other hearts convert,
    And so take up, at use, good store;
That to Thy chests, there might be coming in,
    Both all my praise, and more!"

VII.

THE morning interview left a painful impression on my mind. The frightful delusion, under which Davis had fled to a refuge of lies, was broken indeed; but I greatly feared some other snare might be spread by the Destroyer.

It was with deep solicitude, therefore, that I called in the afternoon. Before reaching his room, I was met by the mother, wearing a joyful countenance, who said:

"Davis will be so glad to see you! A great change has come over him. He has been filled with joy since the middle of the forenoon; and it began in this way. I was sitting beside him, in company with my younger son, when he suddenly exclaimed, 'Oh, mother, Jesus is precious to me ; why, He *is* precious to me. I am so happy ! I wish I could go to Him now ! Don't you see the angels !' And then, at short intervals, he broke out spontaneously, as if looking directly upon the Saviour, 'Precious Jesus ! Precious Jesus !'"

The tidings of this change seemed too good to be true. I could not believe, for joy. Rather, my mind was preoccupied with the scene of the morning. I was afraid, for the moment, that another, and still more subtle and mighty delusion, must be encountered and broken.

I was alarmed at his reference to the angels. He spoke of them as "*big angels*," and seemed to wonder that his mother could not see them. My fear was, that he was about to rely upon visible appearances and wonderful revelations, apart from the Scriptures, as the ground of his hope.

I know that an angel appeared to the holy women at the sepulchre of Jesus. I know that He is Lord of Angels, and can just as easily show to his servants, their glory, as his own. I know that they are "*all* ministering spirits, *sent forth* to minister for them who shall be heirs of salvation," and that they are glad when sinners are brought unto Jesus with tears of penitence. I know too, that Christians of former generations made much more of angelic agency than we do, for I have read "The Ministration of, and Communion with, Angels;" by Isaac Ambrose; and have often heard the venerable Dr. Archibald Alexander pray in the Oratory of Princeton Seminary and elsewhere, with the simplicity of faith, for holy angels to be sent as attendants and guardians. I once witnessed a scene in which an intelligent Christian youth, about to die, startled every one in the room by calling us together around his bed, and exclaiming — his eye that could not see the sun at midday, being intently fixed in an upward gaze—"HUSH! HARK! SPIRIT!" Of all this, and more, relating to the appearance and agency of holy angels about the beds of the dying "heirs of salvation," I have often thought since the time of which I am writing; and I have come to the conclusion not to be alarmed by such references to angels as Davis made, if there are satisfactory proofs that Jesus is seen and trusted and embraced. I do not know that he did not see angels, and "big angels," angels excelling in strength.

But I was alarmed then; I was afraid of some new delusion; and the time was so short. It seemed to me, that the responsibility of guiding this one soul, was greater than I could bear.

As I approached his cot, he received me with great affection and immediately spoke of the change that had taken place in his views and feelings. The ecstasy of his first look at the Person and glory of Christ, had so far subsided, that he could speak calmly and intelligently of his experience; his countenance always fine, even when shaded with the distressing apprehension of deserved wrath, was now lighted up with the joy and peace of a believer, and he expressed very decidedly the hope of pardon and acceptance with God, for the sake of Christ. I asked him the ground of his hope. He replied: "You told me that God was so willing to save me, that He wanted to save me, and that He would save me, if I would stop trying to save myself and trust in the

Saviour; and this I do; there is nothing else I can do."

I then pressed him with many inquiries, to learn how far he had scriptural views of Christ, His Living Person, His offices, and His sacrificial death; and whether he was really drawn to Him, and constrained to receive and rest upon Him alone for salvation, as He is revealed and offered to sinners in the Bible.

I was careful to ask him about his views of sin, whether he adopted God's views, scriptural views of his great sinfulness, of the malignity and vileness of his sins, of the justice of his condemnation on account of them, of his entire helplessness, and of the necessity of his being cleansed from the pollution, as well as delivered from the punishment of his sins, in order to enter heaven; and whether he was looking unto Jesus to do all this for him.

To these inquiries, and to many others, relating to the renewing and sanctifying work of the Holy Spirit, his answers were clear and most satisfactory. From Monday till the hour of this interview, he had been patiently instructed, both in writing and orally, on all the points of evangelical doctrine referred to in these questions; and when the divine illumination came, the shining of God into his soul, he seemed to be translated at once out of darkness into the marvellous light of the gospel. I was compelled to hope that he was indeed taught of God, and to mingle my tears of joy and thanksgiving with those of the mother over her son that was dead and lost, at length, through the infinite mercy of God, made alive and found. And I could easily believe, that whether he saw angels or not, in the first flood of light that reached him from the Person and throne of his Lord, they saw him and rejoiced over him with exceeding great joy. "There is joy in the presence of the angels of God over one sinner that repenteth."

The closing sentence in the record of my visit to Davis, on this occasion, made immediately after returning to my room, was as follows:

"I was almost overpowered with the interview, and with the evidence that his mind had apprehended the great mystery of a free salvation."

Years have passed since that interview. The evidence of his regeneration and union to Christ by the power of the Holy Ghost, accumulating rapidly till he was struck by death, has been often reviewed. I am not wholly ignorant of Satan's devices, nor of the great danger of self-deception, in what are called death-bed repentances.

I believe that many persons, after having

long trampled under foot the precious blood of Christ, and despised His authority and love, are left, at the end, to "strong delusions to believe a lie."

I am sure that our Adversary the Devil has cunning, malignity and power enough, when he is not hindered by Jesus, to transform himself into an angel of light, and stand by the dying sinner, on purpose to lure him to hell, by leading him to think and say he is going to heaven.

And I believe still further that under the influence of disease, some persons apparently go through the successive stages of awakening, conviction, conversion, and rapid sanctification, while they have no true self-control. If they die, they are believed to be safe; but if they recover, they not only give melancholy proof that they are not Christ's, but they retain no recollection whatever of their own professions of attach-

ment to Him, made while they were sick.
Such instances are not unknown in pastoral
experience. Therefore let no one delay
his own application for mercy; it is a vain
and dangerous expectation you cherish, that
you will be inclined and able to come to
Christ, when you are sick and dying.

But now having said all this, I must add,
that I do not believe the case of Davis be-
longs to either of the above classes. It
must be possible for the Holy Spirit to au-
thenticate His own work, when it is a short
work. He that wrought effectually in the
dying malefactor, convincing him of sin,
constraining him to look and cry unto
Jesus, bleeding at his side, and uniting him
for ever to His Person, may still exhibit
in His dealings with sinners about to die,
the power of grace, reigning through righteousness unto eternal life, by Jesus Christ
our Lord.

The following chapters, contain abundant proof, I think, that Davis had become a child of God by the renewing of the Holy Ghost and faith in our Lord Jesus Christ, justifying the strong language of an experienced minister, who often saw him, and whose letter is given later in this volume :

"I doubt not, we coincide in the opinion, that while many, if not most cases, of death-bed repentances are deceptive, this was real."

CHAPTER VIII.

Patient in Tribulation.

"For our light affliction which is but for a moment, worketh for us a far more exceeding and eternal weight of glory; while we look not at the things which are seen, but at the things which are not seen."

PAUL.

"Wherefore should we sigh and languish,
    When our cares so soon shall cease,
And the heart that sows in anguish
    Shall hereafter reap in peace?"

VIII.

I HOPE the reader will not take up the record of this day's experience without a moment's reflection.

It is no imaginary sufferer, or ideal Christian, that lies before you. He is a man subject to like passions with yourself. A thousand ties are binding him to the earth. You probably never saw more manly vigour and beauty in one so young. I know, that you cannot be more tenderly loved by parents, sisters, brothers and friends, and that you cannot more fully reciprocate love, than he; nor can your earthly future be brighter now, than was his at the hour of his hurt. What can you say of the endless future

9

that opens beyond you, and of your preparation for a conscious and accountable
existence, as long as it lasts ?

Davis is very near the grave. Death has
possession already of more than half his
body, while it is fiercely contending for the
rest. He has fearful agonies to bear, before his week is spent, and his endless Sabbath with God comes.

Observe how patiently he suffers; how
serenely he waits upon God; how cheerfully he walks with Jesus his Lord through
the fire kindled to refine him, as silver, and
purify him as gold.

I have seen many Christians of mature
experience, enduring the chastenings of the
Lord, and glorying in tribulation; but I
never saw one, of any age, more truly, in
every way, "an example of suffering affliction, and of patience."

When I called in the morning, I found

him still cheerful and bright. His face beamed with intelligence and contentment, though marks of great suffering had begun to appear. Christ was bearing him tenderly in His arms, as a shepherd a wounded lamb, causing him to know that he was perfectly safe. And he had great need of the humble consciousness of such a relation to the Redeemer, to make him strong for the duties and sufferings of the day.

His Brooklyn physicians, Drs. Mason and Isaacs, had already decided upon a final consultation with Drs. Mott, Carnochan, and Watson, of New York, at four o'clock in the afternoon. The object of this consultation was to ascertain, after a careful examination, whether an operation for restoring the displaced vertebra to its true position, could avail to preserve, or materially prolong his life. I spoke to him of this, and told him frankly, at the request of Dr. Mason, that an operation would not be attempted, unless it was found that nothing else could save him; also, that if it was resorted to, the probabilities were very much against its success; and that it might be attended with instant death.

I could hardly suppose that one so immature in Christian experience, and having so much to make life sweet, would hear this statement without alarm. I therefore tried to fortify him, as far as possible, against the dread of death, by assuring him that Christ would never leave nor forsake him; that He had promised this in a great variety of terms; and that He had been with others who trusted Him, in times of the deepest distress, giving to His faithful martyrs the grace of joyfulness, even when they were dying in the flames and on the rack. But he did not seem to need such comforting suggestions from me. Already he had been led, by the Holy Spirit, into the depths of Divine consolation, and had no fear of the worst that could happen to him. He therefore waited calmly for the hour of the "final consultation," ready to do and suffer the will of his Heavenly Father concerning him.

9*

CHAPTER IX.

Submission.

"OH, MY FATHER, IF THIS CUP MAY NOT PASS AWAY FROM ME, EXCEPT I DRINK IT, THY WILL BE DONE."   JESUS.

"When all created streams are dried,
Thy fulness is the same;
May I with this be satisfied,
And glory in Thy name."

IX.

I went early, and remained with Davis till half-past six o'clock. The Rev. Mr. Janes was there when I arrived. Knowing the fearful ordeal through which Davis was about to pass, he had endeavoured to draw from him a reason for the hope that was in him. The result, as he assured me, was a deep conviction that the sufferer had become a beloved child of God.

Shortly before the physicians met in his room, I asked him if he was willing to trust himself in their hands, knowing, on their authority, that any operation they might decide to perform, would be a last resort, and that the result would probably be in-

stant death? He answered promptly, and
cheerfully, "Yes;" and then added, "I
would a little rather live than die, though I
do not know that I have any choice on my
own account. My parents and friends are
very anxious to have me live, and I would
like to live for their sake; otherwise, I
would quite as soon die. Life is very
short, at longest. I have lived twenty
years, and they are nothing, and if I am
spared now, I must soon die."

In this strain he spoke with great sweet-
ness and liberty. He also expressed the
thought, that he was gaining a wonderful
experience of life, as it were, in a few moments. Frequently, indeed, his mind was
absorbed with this thought; and several
times, he exclaimed, "I seem to be forty
years old." And no marvel. The sudden
interruption of all his earthly plans; his
experience of protracted suffering; the

crowding of numerous friends and ac-
quaintances around him, anxious to minister
to his comfort; and, above all, his new
views of himself as a sinner, of Christ as
his Saviour, and of eternal ·things, revealed
to him in their vastness and power, added
many years to his short life, if years can be
measured by thoughts and experience.

Finding him steadfast and immoveable in
view of death—cheerfully assured that nothing could harm him — I asked him on
what his hopes for eternity rested. He
answered : "Simply on the promise of God.
He always keeps His word." And to many
other questions, meant to assist him in the
work of self-examination, he gave ready and
satisfactory answers. It was a rare privilege to hear him express his love for the
Lord Jesus Christ, and to see him as he
drank in the sweet truths of the gospel.

Expecting every moment to have our

interview broken off, by the arrival of the
physicians, and wishing to give Davis as
much instruction and consolation as possible,
in final preparation for his great trial, Mr.
Janes and myself read and repeated appropriate passages of Scripture, and portions
of hymns, and prayed with him. While we
were thus engaged, he gave himself up,
most intently, to the hearing and reception
of the truth. I thought of him then, and
have often thought of him since, as a living
receptacle for the truth, prepared by God
Himself, "a vessel unto honor sanctified,
and meet for the Master's use." I received
new impressions of the adaptation of truth
to the human soul, and of the power of a
gracious soul to receive and appropriate, or,
if I may use the word, *assimilate* the truth.
His eye was fixed steadily on us, as we
spoke in turn, each suggesting the thoughts
that occurred at the moment, as most im-

portant for him to have in mind. And although these thoughts were drawn from the Scriptures, and we expressed them chiefly in the words of the Holy Ghost,—words, which, in some instances, he had not heard since his experience of the new life—he received them all with indications of intelligence and delight that were surprising.

The words of Holy Writ, "Swift to hear," express the exact truth of the experience I am now describing. He was "swift to hear;" and I think that if there had been any method by which we could have brought much larger portions of the Scriptures before his mind, during the few moments of our interview—such was the gracious aptitude of his soul for divine things—he would have received all, with very little, if any, interpretation on our part.

Shortly after four o'clock, the physicians

came into his room, and proceeded to ex-
amine his neck and spine with great care.
On being raised from a horizontal position,
though he was supported with the utmost
skill of those accustomed to the sick room,
he suffered intensely, and almost fainted.
His pulse went down to twelve. He soon
rallied, however, and bore the examination
with great fortitude.

As Dr. Isaacs moved his fingers down
the spine, toward the small of the back,
there seemed to be faint indications of sensibility; but they were deceptive. The
paralysis was final, and hopeless; and the
surgeons knew that the case was beyond
their skill.

After they retired, and had been in consultation some time, word came to us,—
waiting in painful suspense to know the
result,—that they had decided not to ope-
rate. At this word, and the apparent sen-

sibility along the spine, the mother caught as a straw of hope, and said to Davis, "This is encouraging;" turning to me, with the inquiry, "Do you not think so?" I was compelled to say, that I thought it important to have no impression conveyed to the mind of Davis, regarding his physical condition, except by his physician. And very soon, alas! Mr. Dennis, of the "Atlantic Mutual Insurance Company," told me, with tears, that "all hope was gone; that Davis must die, and die in two or three days, at farthest."

It was a great relief, at the moment, to be assured that, from the nature of his injuiry, his sufferings would not be great; that the paralysis would gradually extend to the parts of his person, still susceptible of feeling, till life was gently extinguished like a dying taper.

The result was far otherwise, in consequence, I suppose, of the remarkable vigour of his constitution.

With the sorrow of his parents when the result of the consultation was known, a stranger intermeddleth not. It fell to my lot to tell them that Davis was soon to die, and to witness their grief. But I cannot speak of it. God was their refuge and strength; they could not have borne the strokes of His hand, but for this; and though they well nigh fainted at first, they were so helped by His grace, as to endure their anguish and conceal it from their son.

In nothing, perhaps, was his cheerful resignation to the will of God more remarkably shown, than in the manner in which he received the report of the physicians. It was communicated to him by a friend of the family, who had left the house while the consultation was in progress, and under the impression that there was some ground of hope for his recovery. She did not return till the result was known. As soon as I told her that Davis could live but two or three days, at most, she sat for a moment almost paralyzed with grief, and then, recovering herself, hurried into his room. We had not yet agreed upon any method of communicating to him the certain knowledge that he must die so soon.

This was God's method; and although at first the mother started to prevent the sudden communication of the sad tidings to her son, there was really no time to hinder it; and we did not regret that he was thus made acquainted with the worst.

In a moment his voice was distinctly heard calling: "Mother! Mother!" As she entered the room she took her place at the head of his cot, and behind him, to conceal her emotions; but he immediately said, "I want you to stand before me,

10*

mother, and look in my face." He then gazed up at her intently and continued:

"Mother! what is this? Have you kept anything from me? Is there no hope? What do they say?"

"No, my darling, there is none; they say you must die;" was the only answer she could give.

Closing his eyes, as if to help the power of thought, he said with great deliberation, "Is—that—so? I find that I have been clinging to hope, more than I thought, BUT IT IS ALL WELL."

Thus sweetly did he bow to his Father's will; there were no tears; there was no rebellion. Having submitted himself to the righteousness of God by the power of the Holy Ghost, renouncing his own will in the most difficult of all the acts of faith—the glad acceptance of Christ as his own Saviour—he found it comparatively easy to yield in everything else.

When I entered the room, I found him trying to calm the grief of the friend who had told him he must die, and talking to her of heaven. He seemed to feel no solicitude about the future for himself, and his chief concern now was to persuade her to prepare for death.

He begged her to come to Christ at once, that she might be ready to leave the world at any moment. He tried to tell her just what she must do to be saved. "Only believe," he said; "just believe what the Bible tells you; this is all I have done; I was told to believe on the Lord Jesus Christ, and God would receive me, and He has received me."

"But, Davis, you are good and I am not," was her answer; "I have never thought of God; I have lived in the midst of gaiety."

With great seriousness he said :

"I am not good. Why, I am not good; but I believe what God says, and then I just shut my eyes and think, and the angels are all about me, to carry me to heaven. I have had evil thoughts and feelings twenty years; I have bad thoughts still; I am not a Christian."

This last remark was made apparently under the impression, that a real Christian was free from sin, while he was painfully conscious of his depravity. But when I explained to him that he was a Christian, if he trusted and loved the Saviour, he was satisfied.

As this conversation progressed, Davis occasionally appealed to me to confirm the sentiments he expressed, thus giving me the opportunity to speak to both, some of the precious truths of the Bible, that were suited to guide their souls into paths of peace; and so absorbed was he in the conversation, that I am persuaded he did not dwell painfully upon the tidings so lately brought to him about his death.

After a while, however, he turned his eye to a Christian friend, who felt deeply for him, and asked:

"Did you ever see any one die?"

She told him that she had seen several persons die. He then asked further:

"Are you afraid to die?" She answered, "No!" and immediately asked in turn: "Davis, are you afraid to die?" He replied at once:

"No! I am not afraid to die, but somehow I dread the last struggle."

And I know that the fear, even of dying, was more and more taken away, until at last he watched his changing pulse with seeming pleasure, and was obliged to seek grace, to wait all the days of his appointed time, rather than dying grace. With many friends holding him to the earth, and the Lord of glory drawing him heavenward, he was in a strait betwixt two; but his prevalent desire was to depart, and be with Christ, which was far better.

Something led me to ask him at this interview, if he would like to leave any word with me, for the young men associated with him in the Company, by which he was employed.

With much feeling he said, the tears flowing down his cheeks, though he had not wept at any time under his own physical distresses, and did not weep for himself in the near prospect of death :

"Tell them to take warning from me. Tell them not to put off preparation for death, for they know not the hour, when the Son of Man cometh. I might have been killed in an instant. Only think of the mercy of God to me, but they may not have time to prepare for death." And then he continued: "I have often been to funerals and heard what was spoken, just as I have heard preaching in the church, without caring to understand and to remember."

He was anticipating their attendance upon his funeral services, and fearing that they might hear in vain even then.

After this, his mind reverted to the certainty and nearness of his death; and he expressed the fear, that he was not troubled enough about dying. On this point he made very particular inquiries of me, remarking that he had been so many years a great sinner that it seemed wonderful he should be now dying, and yet have no fear.

It is well for the reader to search for the ground of this peace. Davis was calm and often exultant, while he knew that death was steadily approaching, and had come almost to his cot. And he found all his joy and peace in believing. He was shocked by the review of his life; he saw only a mass of sin. "For twenty years," he said, "I have done nothing but sin." This was the honest confession that more than once fell from his lips; and yet he had peace with God through our Lord Jesus Christ. Moreover this profound peace was attended by a painful sense of the vileness of sin; he loathed himself, while he clung to Christ; he clung to Christ, because he loathed himself; he could do nothing else. When told that he need not be afraid to think of his sins, and that he ought to confess them, he said that he had no reason or wish, to hide them, but was glad God knew them all. Still they grieved him to the heart. This was apparent from the hour of his espousals to

Christ, and there were times when it seemed
as if his soul would faint under the discovery of indwelling sin. "Oh," he exclaimed, during the affecting interview of
which this is a very imperfect account, "I
have wicked thoughts now, how shall I get
rid of them?"

Thus the Holy Spirit revealed to him
more and more the plague of his heart, and
the all-sufficiency and nearness of Christ.
Up to the close of this day, he seemed always to have the glorious Person of the
Redeemer in full view. But a new experience awaited him. The early hours of
Friday, were marked by the hiding of the
Saviour's face.

CHAPTER X.

FRIDAY MORNING, JULY 24

Dark Hours.

"ELOI, ELOI, LAMA SABACHTHANI?"

JESUS ON THE CROSS.

"But, O MY GOD! MY GOD! why leab'st thou me,
Thy Son, in whom thou dost delight to be?
MY GOD! MY GOD!

Neber was grief like mine."

X.

I WAS sent for at five o'clock in the morning, in consequence of a season of great conflict and darkness, through which Davis was called to pass. The Rev. Mr. Janes, who lived just at hand, had been called an hour before, and was the happy instrument, before my arrival, of leading the sufferer back to the path of peace.

The following letter contains his account, of what he appropriately calls, "the temptation by which Mr. Johnson was assailed," and of the method of his deliverance. This view, however, is perfectly consistent with the idea, that the progress of disease was intimately connected with the dark hours,

11*

that cast their shadows over his soul. We are fearfully and wonderfully made. The maladies that vitiate our blood, and shatter our nerves, make it impossible, sometimes, for even the Christian of longest experience, to find and enjoy his Beloved.

　　　　　　　　　"New York, February 20, 1860.

"Rev. J. D. Wells :

　　"*Dear Brother:*—In reply to your note of the 13th inst., I will say, that I kept no memorandum of my visits to the bed-side of the lamented young Mr. Johnson. As near as I recollect, the point of the temptation by which he was assailed, at the time to which you refer, was,—that he had no right to hope for heaven, as he had done nothing for the Saviour on earth; and that it would be dishonourable for him to receive in death, the mercy and salvation of that God, whose claims he had disregarded in life; and this awakened in him the desire to live long enough to do something for God.

"I reminded him that faith is the Bible condition of salvation, and not works; and that were he to live a thousand years, and keep the commandments to the best of his ability, still it would be necessary for him, in order to be saved, to cast himself, as a helpless sinner, by penitence and faith, upon the mercy of God, through the merits of Christ. I reminded him that he had already done this, and had found pardon and peace; and that he must continue to rely upon Christ, alone, for salvation, for a few hours longer, and he should be saved; for God had said, 'He that believeth shall be saved.'

"This view of the plan of salvation (which, in the hour of conflict, he had lost sight of), seemed to break the force of the temptation, and he was enabled to replace his wavering faith upon the atonement, and centre his hope of heaven upon his Redeemer.

"I then sought to engage his mind, by quoting passages of Scripture, descriptive of the sufferings of Christ, and his invitations to the sinner, to share in the benefits of those sacrificial sufferings. I also quoted, slowly, and at intervals, as he was able to listen, the hymn, beginning with 'Jesus, lover of my soul,' and at each succeeding moment, the power of temptation was weakened, and the power of faith increased, until he was enabled firmly to trust, and calmly to wait, for a happy immortality.

"Dear brother, I have no 'suggestions' to make. I was impressed, at the time of the funeral, that, in your discourse, you gave a faithful account of that dying seeker, and a correct analysis of his experience.

"I cannot question the propriety of giving publicity to this extraordinary case, in which the grace of God is so marvellously exhibited.

"I doubt not, we coincide in the opinion, that while many, if not most cases of death-bed repentance, are deceptive, this was real.

"Yours, in the fellowship of the gospel,

"E. L. JANES."

It was a great mercy to Davis that he enjoyed the counsels of one skilled in the blessed ministry of truth, in the time of his distress. When told that he had only to be willing to receive Christ as his Saviour, and to rest upon Him alone for salvation, he asked with great eagerness, as I was informed by one who was present, "Is that all?" and added immediately, "I am willing, I am willing." And thus ended the temptation, never to be renewed. Again the Beloved stood revealed at his side. For a small moment He had forsaken His young disciple, but with everlasting kindness He returned to him again; and taking him to His arms, He carried him in His bosom, as long as we were permitted to accompany him.

Till his death, Davis never regretted these dark hours. They were often referred to; they gave him a profound and affecting interest in the mysterious sufferings of Christ on the cross, under the weight of which he cried out: "Eloi, Eloi, lama Sabachthani? which is, being interpreted, My God, My God, why hast thou forsaken me?"

They brought him into sympathy with a multitude of believers, who have been compelled to lament and confess with David, Ps. xxxviii. 3, 4, "There is no soundness in my flesh, because of thine anger; neither is there any rest in my bones, because of my sin. For mine iniquities are gone over mine head; as a heavy burden they are too heavy for me."

But he could also add with them, in the hour of his deliverance, Ps. xl. 1, 2, "I waited patiently for the LORD, and he inclined unto me, and heard my cry. He brought me up also out of a horrible pit, out of the miry clay, and set my feet upon a rock, and established my goings."

They gave him breadth of experience, wonderfully increasing his capacity for receiving instruction and comfort from portions of the Scriptures, which he could not have understood, under the discipline of physical suffering only.

There was no difficulty in his embracing those humbling truths, which the natural man receiveth not; the desperate wickedness of the heart; the pollution of sin; the entire helplessness of the sinner; the necessity of our being sought and saved by Christ, through the instrumentality of the truth, and by the power of the Holy Ghost; and our absolute dependence upon the grace of the Redeemer for every moment's continuance in the path of life.

When I reached the house, Davis had come out of the conflict, and was resting on Christ as before; but he was suffering fearfully for want of breath, and from extreme prostration and nervousness. He could not bear to have a loud word spoken in the room; the powers of life sunk so low in a few moments, that we thought him dying, and he evidently thought himself, that he was about to leave us.

"Put your arms round my neck," he said to his mother; "take my head in your arms, I am going to sleep. Good-bye

father; good-bye mother; good-bye Lonny"
(his brother Alonzo), and thus he continued
till he had taken leave of every one present.
We all bade him good-bye, and commended
him to God in prayer. But he soon rallied
again, and continued to suffer indescribable
pains. Indeed the entire day was one of
agony for want of breath, his lungs being
partially paralyzed, and the paralysis con-
stantly extending; and, in consequence of
this impaired respiration, he became so prostrated, as to suffer acutely from exhaus-
tion. "I am so tired, oh, I am so tired,"
he would exclaim, scores of times in succes-
sion, though without any signs of impa-
tience. Once, as he opened his mouth and
panted, his broad chest heaving in the effort
to get his lungs filled with air, he said, with
an expression of anguish never to be forgotten by those who saw it, "I would be

willing to suffer again all that I have borne, if I could get one good breath."

It was his earnest desire to be released from his misery by death. "Is it wrong for me, not to drink water when I want it?" he asked; "I should die without it; would it be right for me to hasten my death in this way?" This question revealed at once his agony, and his purpose to wait for death. I need hardly say that the water he drank, was always thrown from his stomach in a few moments, as pure almost as when he received it.

He was not unmindful, during this day of ineffable distress, of the kind offices of those who ministered to his necessities. "I thank you!" he exclaimed, calling some of us by name; "it was very wicked in me, not to think of it before."

My record of this interview, made at the time, closed with these words: "I could write a volume almost from the experience of to-day, from 5 o'clock in the morning till half past one o'clock in the afternoon, when I left to return to-night."

At this distance of time, I shall not trust my memory to add to the account already given, but proceed with the record made of his last night.

CHAPTER XI.

"The Furnace of Affliction."

"BEHOLD THY SON. * * * BEHOLD THY MOTHER."
JESUS ON THE CROSS.

"What though the tempest rage,
　　Heaven is my home;
Short is my pilgrimage,
　　Heaven is my home;
Time's cold and wintry blast,
Soon will be over past,
I shall reach home at last,
　　Heaven is my home."

12*

XI.

IT was my great privilege to be with Davis during the whole of this night, and until eleven o'clock Saturday morning.

There were three other watchers; and some idea of his physical condition may be formed from the fact, that it required the undivided attention of four men to minister to him. Two had charge of his arms, and two were needed to care for his head and neck.

The entire night was spent in extreme suffering. Occasionally, it became necessary to raise his head, that the air might pass between it and the pillow, to cool the burning heat, and give a moment's relief to the dislocated neck. But this was a work of great difficulty, requiring the combined skill and efforts of all the watchers, with the consent and direction of the sufferer himself.

The scene, precisely as it was then en-acted, has often presented itself to my mind since that night. I have thought of the labor it cost us, to mitigate for a moment, and to the least degree, the distress of our dying friend. I have thought, too, of the rich man's request, that Lazarus might be sent from the bosom of Abraham, to dip the tip of his finger in water, and cool his tongue. It has seemed to me very dread-ful to bear, or even witness, the sufferings of the present time, when all that medical skill, and the tenderest devotion of love, can do for their relief, is faithfully done. And yet, Jesus bids us not to fear the suf-ferings of time; not to fear even those enemies that have power to kill the body, and after that, have no more that they can do. But, at the same time, He forewarns us whom we shall fear, "Fear Him," He says, "who, after He hath killed, hath power to cast into hell. Yea, I say unto you, fear Him."

I beg the reader to look thoughtfully on this scene, remembering that the principal person in it is a beloved child of God, and most dear to many hearts, for his own sake, and for Christ's sake. He asks us to move his head. Immediately every watcher takes his appointed place. One stands at each side, to raise the arm and shoulder. Another kneels at his head, with his hands gently, but firmly, thrust down almost to the fracture in the neck. The fourth is ready for any service to which he may be called. And now the word is given by the sufferer himself. He needs great fortitude, great confidence in his attendants, and, above all, great trust in his Saviour, to give it, for he is sure to suffer, and may die in our hands. But, with a cheerful voice, that helps us in our work, he says, deliberately, "Now lift," at the same time yielding himself to us. If we begin precisely together, and do not change the relative position of his head and body, we succeed in raising him so far, that his pillow can be drawn carefully out and turned, while the fan is used to relieve, for a moment, the great heat of his head and neck. And then, with the utmost caution, he is allowed to sink down to his place again.

Does the reader imagine, that he could be in such a case, with no hope or possibility of relief, just about to encounter the King of terrors, and yet carry forward, successfully, the neglected work of seeking Christ and salvation?

But look, still further, at the sufferings of Davis, as the last long night given him for the trial of his hopes, wore away.

There was intense wakefulness, an entire inability to sleep, with the feeling that the power of thinking, was beyond his control. There was no mental aberration; but the stimulus supplied the brain seemed to be excessive, and the mind could get no repose. There was no perceptible relief, even during the "sinking turns," when his pulse was a flutter, and the soul seemed ready to depart.

Again, at intervals, there were spasms of extreme sensibility in the wrists and palms of the hands. For the most part during this last night, the sensation in his arms and hands was that of numbness; they felt as if they were asleep, and it was a great relief to have them rubbed and pressed with the hand, and sometimes very briskly excited with a stiff flesh brush. But in an instant, and frequently, the shattered nerves losing their partial insensibility, became so sensitive as not to bear the slightest touch.

Besides this, there was the ever increasing agony of impeded respiration. Paralysis was creeping through the lungs, and shutting out the vital air, so that the sufferer was forced to distend his mouth to the utmost, gasping and panting for breath, and often crying out in the greatness of his agony.

Nor was this all. I have spoken before, of the prostration of strength consequent upon his inability to inflate his lungs; this steadily increased till the piteous exclamation: "Oh, I am so tired," was repeated hundreds of times.

And still further, there was the aching of his shoulders, and sometimes acute pains in his neck, so fearfully fractured.

And to all this there must be added, raging thirst, that could not be slaked. We were giving him iced water at short intervals all night, and removing the cloths upon which it was thrown shortly after he had received it.

Here, then, was a remarkable combination of distresses, any one of which was enough to tax the powers of human endurance to the utmost. Nothing but the pleasant assurance of the sufferer's union to Christ, and nearness to heaven, enabled us to witness his agony with composure. But as the case stood, I watched all his changing symptoms, as well as the attitude of his mind towards the Saviour, with an interest amounting almost to fascination. It was really wonderful, to witness the conflict between the vital power in his noble frame, and death. Again and again, when the victory seemed about to be gained by the destroyer, he was driven away, and life reigned once more, enthroned, to appearance, as firmly as ever.

But I must speak of other things that occupied our attention, during the night. Davis was tenderly devoted to his mother. He loved to have her near him. Indeed, she was the only person that he would allow, to sit or stand before him for any time, looking into his face. He shrunk instinctively from being a spectacle to be gazed at, either in pity or wonder; and he more than once requested persons to leave the room, or go behind him; but always in such a way as to give no offence. And yet, as often as his mother appeared, his beautiful face beamed with pleasure. No hands were so pleasant about his face, as hers. But his delight in her was so unselfish, that he would not consent to her remaining long with him at a time. She was much worn by constant watching, and needed rest. As often, therefore, as he sent her away from his presence into the adjoining room, he extorted the promise, that she would lie down and try to sleep. At the same time he promised to send for her, when he wished her to come to his bed-side.

This was his own arrangement for the night. And, four times I think, before the day broke, he asked that she might be called. On each of these occasions we were compelled to witness the same affecting scene, retreating as far as possible to hide our tears, and prevent his hearing our sobs. When his mother came in, he immediately asked her to put her head down and kiss him, not waiting for her to do it of her own accord. He seemed to be eager for this embrace of pure love. At the same time he requested us to lift his arms, and put them around his mother; for, though they still retained a measure of sensibility and obeyed his will, it was too great a trial of his strength to move them far. And holding her in his arms, he would kiss her lips again and again, as if drinking thus the very love of her heart. " Oh, if you could could go with me," he said at one of these interviews, " how sweet to be together." And then, rallying, before the thought of their temporary separation had become overwhelming to her and himself, he added : " Never mind, it won't be long."

Each of these interviews was marked by the utmost cheerfulness on his part; he did not shed a tear; and for his sake, his mother was enabled to repress her emotions, so as not to weep; but we who were of necessity witnesses of the scene, were compelled to weep like children. Nor was it easy to recover our self-possession after they were separated, because of his frank declaration of filial love, " Oh, I do love my mother so;" words that seemed to be his apology to us for the tax he could not but see he was imposing upon our sensibilities.

It may be properly mentioned in this connection, as a mark of his good breeding not only, but of his delicate Christian sensibility, that he was very mindful of the attention shown him.

At one time, as I was wiping his face, and removing cloths, upon which he had thrown water from his mouth, he said : " It is very kind in you to do this for me—it must be very unpleasant." I assured him, that it was far otherwise, that I accounted it a great privilege to be with him, and to do anything for his relief; and then I reminded him that Jesus washed His disciples' feet. This last suggestion strongly arrested his attention, and afforded him a subject of pleasant thought.

He could not bear much conversation

13*

during this last night of his life. For this reason, it was only now and then that anything was said to him directly upon the subject of his relations to the Saviour, and his prospects for the eternal future. But he was uniformly calm. He watched, with the liveliest interest, the state of his pulse, and all the indications of the approach of death.

Once he lifted up his arms as high as he could, and cried out (for he was in great agony), "Oh, that He would let me put my arms around His neck, and come to Him now." I asked, "Do you mean the Saviour, Davis?" "Of course, I do," was his quick, and very emphatic answer. This cry to the Saviour was wholly spontaneous. It was prompted by nothing said to him; and it occurred when we did not know that his thoughts were occupied with anything but his sufferings. Even then, he was looking unto Jesus, gazing steadfastly into heaven. To his faith, the Lord of glory was a real, living, and accessible Person, with His two natures inseparable. He could not quite reach Him with his extended arms, or he would have embraced Him in the holy familiarity of a love surpassing the love he had for his mother. But he could, and did stretch out his arms, those poor arms, in which so much of the life in his dying body remained, and ask that the Saviour would let him come home then.

And his cry was heard.

CHAPTER XII.

SATURDAY AFTERNOON, JULY 25.

Faithful unto Death.

"Be thou faithful unto death, and I will give thee a crown of life." JESUS in glory.

"So closely are we link'd in love,
So wholly one with Thee,
That all THY bliss and glory then,
Our bright reward shall be."

XII.

AT eleven o'clock A. M., I very reluctantly left Davis, to get some rest, preparatory to my work on the Sabbath. As I parted with him, I kissed him good-bye, and told him how unwillingly I went. The reader must indulge the freedom of my narrative. I was parting with one who, I believed, had become, through grace, an heir of glory, and a beloved brother, an eternal brother in Christ. It was, therefore, grateful to my feelings, to greet him with "a kiss of charity," and to have him assure me, that he fully appreciated the necessity for my absence; and, the more so, because he had expressed a desire to

die, having his mother and father and myself with him.

Leaving the request, that I might be
sent for immediately, when the change
came, I withdrew, admiring, and, I hope,
adoring the matchless grace that had
abounded towards this dear young man,
through Jesus Christ. I could not but
review the known history of God's dealings
with him. The first fact, in that short
history, has not been given. It was referred to on an earlier page (page **23**), but
reserved for this place.

It was this. On Monday, preceding
the Saturday of his fatal injury, Davis
visited his mother. Drawing a low otto-
man near her, he sat down at her feet, and
resting his head in her lap, as he was wont
to do, he said, "What do you suppose
brought me over?"

"You wanted to see your mother, I presume," was the natural answer.

"No!" he said, "that is not just it. I went to church last night, in Brooklyn, and heard some of the old hymns and tunes, that we used to sing when we were all together, in our own church. This made me feel very solemn. I thought a great deal about you. I was in such a hurry to see you, that I could hardly wait for the day to pass. Are you going out to-night?"

His mother asked if he wished her to go out with him; when he answered, "Oh no! I want you to stay home, that we may be alone and talk."

This was their last evening together, before he was brought home to die. They had much conversation on the subject, so eagerly introduced by himself. He could hardly tell what it was in the hymns and tunes that moved him, except that the associations of earlier years, when the family were together, and all worshipped in the same sanctuary, were powerfully revived.

But there was something more than this. Later inquiry has led to the knowledge of the facts. On the night referred to—Sabbath, July 12—Davis heard a very impressive sermon, in a Baptist church, on the subject of DEATH and ETERNITY.

It was observed, by the Christian friends with whom he sat, that he was unusually attentive and serious throughout the entire service. They spoke of this to each other, several days before he was hurt.

His interest in the service was at its height, I presume, when some familiar hymns were sung to favourite tunes, which he had loved to sing, in other circumstances. It was natural, therefore, that his mind should fasten upon that part of the service, in which he had come to the consciousness of serious thought, and that he should speak to his mother, of that only. But the truth was, he had been deeply impressed by the word of God. The faithful instructions received in the family, and in the Sabbath School of the Reformed Protestant Dutch Church, of which his father was long a Ruling Elder, and his mother a member, had prepared him for the awakening, of which, though he knew it not, he was the subject. In anticipation of his last terrible week, appointed for the development and consummation of the work of grace in his heart, he was aroused to serious thought about death and eternity. And so thorough and abiding was the arrest God had laid upon him, that six days after, he was carrying out his plan, not only to put himself, again, under the same sanctuary influences, but to take his younger brother with him.

To this fact, of earlier date than the facts of my narrative, I am sure, thoughtful

minds will attach great importance.   It was
distinctly before my mind, as I reviewed
the dispensations of God's providence and
grace towards Davis, on the occasion of my
leaving him, shortly before his death.   Indeed, it was the first, and a principal fact,
in the review.   I regarded it as the revelation of a plan of mercy, in which both
the severity and goodness of God, towards
a child of the covenant, had been wonderfully illustrated.   From Saturday night, till
Wednesday noon, he had lain, most of the
time, consciously exposed to the wrath of
God.   No arguments, or assurance, could
convince him that there was any possibility
of his escaping the righteous punishment of
his sins.   For a few hours, on Wednesday
morning, he had given himself up to the
fatal and cheerless delusion, that, after
enduring the torments of the lost in hell,
he knew not how long, he might be released

from prison, through the mercy of God, reaching him in some unrevealed way, and received into heaven. But prayer was made without ceasing for him, and the mighty truths of the gospel, Christ, the wisdom of God, and the power of God, to every one that believeth, were used to save him from death.

Such was the rapid review. And I was now leaving him, as I fully believed, and as many sober-minded Christians, and Christian ministers believed, a living member of Christ's body, a child and heir of God. He was just at the end of his earthly course; but he was also close to the gates of the Eternal City. His hope had been tried by fierce temptations and fearful pains. The graces of the Holy Spirit had been wonderfully matured in his heart, and illustrated in his short Christian life, and many persons had been led to glorify God on his behalf.

14*

Why should I not then rejoice over him, with unspeakable joy? I gave myself up to the tide of emotions, that poured through my heart, and,—if it be a weakness to weep in such circumstances,—to the weakness of many tears.

I had hardly slept when the final message to make haste, if I wished to see Davis alive, reached me at half past two o'clock, P. M.

He was dying. Already his countenance was changed, and his eyes shut forever upon the countenances of his friends. In the terrible conflict, that we had watched so closely for a whole week, death was getting the victory, but we all deeply felt that the sting of death, which is sin, had been extracted by his Lord, and that he was gaining a safe and glorious triumph.

He retained his hold upon Christ, up to the last moment of consciousness, remaining calm, and collected, and trustful. There were no clouds. His last words were, " I AM IN A STRANGE PLACE; WHERE HAVE YOU TAKEN ME? I MUST GET HOME." And thus, in the utterance of a sentiment, ever true in regard to the heirs of salvation, his mind let go its hold upon earthly things.

He died at 3 o'clock, P. M., of Saturday the 25th of July, 1857; his father holding his right hand, and his mother his left hand, while it was my privilege to support his head.

He did not know, perhaps, that his wish, with regard to the circumstances of his death, was gratified. I was thankful to be be so near him; and I here record my gratitude for the unspeakable privilege of walking with this suffering member of the Redeemer's body, through all his Christian course, and quite down to the river of death.

CHAPTER XIII.

Sown in Corruption.

"O Death! where is thy sting?
O Grave! where is thy victory?"

                                        PAUL

———— —— ————

"God, my Redeemer, lives,
    And often from the skies
Looks down and watches all my dust,
    Till he shall bid it rise.

Arrayed in glorious grace,
    Shall these vile bodies shine;
And every shape and every face,
    Look heavenly and divine."

XIII.

THE post-mortem examination was made on Sabbath morning, by the same eminent surgeons who had done everything possible to human skill, to save the life of Davis.

The result is given in their own words, as written by the lamented Dr. Isaacs. To this report of the examination, I think, great importance should be attached; not only because the injury itself was one of rare occurrence, but also and more particularly, because every one can see how marvellous it was, that death did not follow the injury on the instant.

"Post Mortem Examination of the Body of Davis Johnson, Jr.

" The sixth Cervical Vertebra being the seat of the injury,

" We found a small amount of extravasated blood between the muscles, and also on the outer surface of the laminæ of the vertebra. A fracture extended on each side of the spinous process through the laminæ of the vertebra three-fourths of an inch, so as to separate the spinous process and a large portion of the laminæ of the vertebra, constituting a separate portion, which was forced in upon the spinal cord to the depth of three-sixteenths of an inch.

" No blood was extravasated within the spinal canal.

" On opening the dura mater, the cord appeared enlarged, softened, slightly discoloured, and contained minute points of extravasated blood.

"On examining the body of the vertebra, it was broken through and comminuted, being divided into three separate portions."

Thus it appears that the injured vertebra was broken into three principal parts, and that one at least of these three parts was "comminuted," or broken into smaller pieces.

Who does not wonder that he lived a whole week, and such a week! God had given him a remarkable frame, more perfectly developed than any other I ever saw, of the same years. It was overflowing with life; and not till the end for which it was made had been secured, could he die. Then the fountains of his nature were suddenly broken up, and in a few moments his soul was poured out unto death.

The funeral services were at the house in Washington Place, where a prayer was offered among the mourners by the Rev. Mr. Janes; and also at the Presbyterian Church, corner of South Third and Fifth Streets, where the same faithful brother kindly assisted me.

A simple narrative of the principal facts in the experience of Davis, was given to a very large assembly; and these facts, viewed in the light of God's word, were used for the comfort of mourners; the warning of those not reconciled to God, and especially of those to whom Davis had sent messages of warning; and for the instruction of all. The change wrought in his condition, his character, and his prospects for eternity, was claimed as a triumph of Christianity; a change impossible, except to the grace and power of the Holy Ghost, working faith in the sinner's heart, and thereby uniting his person to the Person of Christ in his effectual calling. And this

change was shown to have occurred in connection with the persistent use of the Scriptures, and the fervent intercessions of God's
people.

It was an impressive sight when that
great congregation was set in motion, and
passed in solemn procession by the open
coffin, to look upon the beautiful features
of the dead. More than half an hour was
spent in this way, and many tears were
dropped, even by those who had no personal
connexion or acquaintance with Davis and
his family.

It was our common wish to postpone the
interment of the body until Monday morning, leaving it in the church over night.
But this was found impracticable, because
of incipient and rapid decomposition, and
we were compelled to carry the remains at
once to Greenwood. Already the face,
upon the faithful representative of which

you have looked in the front of this volume, was growing dark with corruption. We were glad that God had provided a place in the bosom of the earth, where we might bury our dead; but none of our hopes, which sustained us at the parting, were buried with him. We believe that the soul of our beloved, made perfect in holiness, passed immediately into glory, and that his body being still united to Christ, rests in the grave until the resurrection.

As in our husbandry, that which we sow is not quickened, except it die, so in God's. First the dying, and then the quickening, of the seed. We mourn at the graves of our friends, though we are sure they are fallen asleep in Jesus. But we remember to our joy, that the decay, the beginning of which we see before the burial, is the pledge of a glorious harvest; it is the dying, that precedes and promises the quickening. We waited, therefore, hopefully, till in the same resurrection of life, all that are Christ's, shall come from the sea and the grave, in the perfected likeness of their Lord.

We go home from the grave to witness and feel, the desolation of death. If time does not blunt the edge of our sorrow, the balm of the Comforter heals our wounds, and we learn after long years of patience under the rod of our Father, that He is pursuing the best, if not the only way, to bring us to Himself.

15*

CHAPTER XIV.

LATER DAYS.

The Voice of Warning.

"He being dead, yet speaketh."   Paul.

"To-day—thy merry heart may feast
On herb, and fruit, and bird, and beast;
To-morrow—spite of all thy glee,
The hungry worms may feast on thee.

"To-morrow! mortal, boast not thou
Of time and tide that are not now!
But think, in one revolving day,
That e'en thyself may pass away."

XIV.

It seemed to me a very serious thing, that I had been entrusted by Davis, with a tender and solemn warning for his associates. Many of them were present at the funeral service, and heard the words of his affecting message. But I feared that even they might have heard with distracted minds; while others, who were not present, might never hear, unless I could speak to them separately, man by man.

I was thus led, after corresponding with one of the officers of the "Atlantic Mutual Insurance Company,"—who cordially approved of the plan, and assumed the expense of carrying it out,—to prepare a letter, to be printed and given to each of the young gentlemen with whom Davis was associated in business. This letter was not distributed as a circular, but sent as a communication directly from myself; and I believe it reached every person for whom it was prepared. It is now published below, in the hope that God may own it as the instrument of good to some who have never seen it, and that in this way, at least, Davis, though dead, may yet speak to the living :

"BREWSTER'S STATION, PUTNAM Co., N. Y.,
"August 6th, 1857.

"MY DEAR SIR :

"The death of your late associate in the office (DAVIS JOHNSON, JR.), has thrown upon me a sacred duty, which I hasten to discharge, though absent from home. If Davis had left only a farewell message for you,—words of kind remembrance and long adieu, charging me with his message,—regard for the living and the dead, would prompt me to bear it to you as soon as possible.

"But the case is far more urgent and affecting. I wish it were in my power to tell you, face to face, what I must make known very imperfectly, in this way. DAVIS did not forget you; nor did he think of earthly ties only, and the sudden interruption of the relations between you and himself. On the borders of eternity, and aroused to intense thoughtfulness on subjects in which he had felt but little interest through life, he was deeply concerned to have you see the things that he saw, and think as he thought, of the relative importance of time and eternity. Hence the solemn and earnest message with which he entrusted me, and which I beg you to receive as from the lips and heart of your dying companion:

"'*Tell them*,' he said, '*to take warning from me. Tell them not to put off preparation for death, for they know not the hour when the Son of Man cometh. I might have been killed in an instant. Only think of the mercy of the Lord to me; but they may not have time to prepare for death.*' And then he continued : '*I have often been to funerals and heard what was spoken, just as I have heard preaching in the church, without caring to understand and remember.*'

"You catch his idea. He was afraid his message might come to you in vain. He knew from experience the greatness of your danger, and therefore alluded to himself. And let me add, that, in sending this message, he was moved to tears. It is due as well to him as yourselves, that I mention, briefly, the circumstances in which his thoughts were turned to his associates in the office.

"He was injured, you know, in the evening of Saturday, July 18th. Up to Wednesday morning following, he was in great mental anguish. His physical distress, from the nature of his injuries, must have been inexpressibly great; but the agony of his mind was greater. He felt and said, when first told that his life was in danger, that he could not die. He bitterly lamented his sins, and, when urged to pray, replied, that he could not pray, for God knew that nothing but his danger would prompt him to cry for mercy. He condemned himself, and justified God without any qualification, owning that he was lost for ever, and deserved to perish. This he said of his own accord, speaking without reserve of his whole life as a life of sin. 'For twenty years,' he said, with anguish depicted in his face, 'I have sinned against God in thought and feeling, in word and act, and it

16

is not possible for me to be saved.' I mention this particularly, that you may mark the change in his estimate of his own character, and see, with him, how little it avails in our approach to eternity, to have the approbation of the world; and also that you may learn the true meaning and value of his dying message.

"I must add, however, that having the common and fatal notion that he must do something to please God, and make Him willing to forgive his innumerable sins, and knowing that he had no time for this, DAVIS was thrown into the depths of despair. It seemed impossible to get his eye fixed upon the Saviour. Many that loved him were chiefly anxious for this. His physicians, and some of his friends from your office, I know, were of this number. It was not till Wednesday, however, that he was enabled to look steadily, and with hope, to the Lord Jesus Christ. In the forenoon of that day, he discovered (there is reason to believe) that eternal life is the gift of God, through Jesus Christ our Lord, and that God can be just in justifying the ungodly who believe in Jesus. And need I tell you, that this wonderful discovery, which no one can make without the illumination of the Holy Spirit, was connected with instant relief to his mind? He was cheered with hope, and had great peace, with very few interruptions, from that time till he died on Saturday, the 25th of July. For an hour or two on Friday morning, his soul was in great darkness; but he emerged from it joyfully, when he discovered again that the Saviour was able and willing to deliver him from his sins, and that he had only to put his trust in Him. The fear of death was taken away, and even when the last hope of recovery was cut off, he remained calm, though all around him were melted to tears.

"Now, my dear sir, it was at the interview I had with your fellow-clerk, after the surgeons had decided that nothing could save, or greatly prolong his life, and when he knew that he must die, that he thought and spoke, of you and your associates; and though he did not weep for himself, he did weep for those to whom he sent words of warning and entreaty. His message was dictated amid tears of tenderness and anxiety. And he did not send it by me alone. I, myself, heard him say to one of your own number, ministering kindly at his bedside: 'C——, talk to the boys in the office, when you get a chance, won't you?' And I know that he left a message with one of the officers of the company for you. This shows a mind intent upon your good. He earnestly desired your salvation.

"In conclusion, therefore, I beg you to hear his voice. Though dead, he yet speaketh. His words are words of soberness and truth. And can you doubt that the hand of God was in his sudden removal, and that the mercy of God sends back to you from his lips, and from the very shadows of eternity, a call to penitence and faith. If you believe already, you will hear this message of your brother, as the voice of your Master, calling you to watchfulness and prayer. Look at the vacant place from which DAVIS has gone for ever, and recall his solemn and earnest words, and look with him unto Jesus, who asks, and deserves, your confidence and love. Do not think me officious, dear sir, if I add, with a profound conviction of the importance of the counsel, and an earnest desire for your salvation: *Search the Scriptures; pray in secret; remember the Sabbath day,*

16*

to keep it holy; reverence the sanctuary; believe on the Lord Jesus Christ, and thou shalt be saved. He that believeth on Him is not condemned: he that believeth not is condemned already, because he hath not believed in the name of the only begotten Son of God.

"I shall be very happy to communicate with you further, if you wish it, either by letter, or at my house, No. 92 South Third Street, Williamsburgh, L. I.

"Sincerely yours,

"J. D. WELLS."

Results are with God. To us it is given, in imitation of our Master, to work the works of Him that sent us, while it is day. The divine promises are our heritage, and they never fail. "Cast they bread upon the waters, for thou shalt find it after many days." "He that goeth forth and weepeth, bearing precious seed, shall doubtless come again with rejoicing, bringing his sheaves with him." It is pleasant to "come" soon, after the sowing. But the joy of this harvest, is mingled with fear, and marred by frequent disappointments. We must wait, in hope, for the harvest at the end of the world. Then we shall enter into the joy of our Lord, the joy that He has, as Lord of the garnered harvest, and learn something of the meaning, hid now, in the wonderful words : "And they that be wise shall shine as the brightness of the firmament, and they that turn many to righteousness, as the stars for ever and ever."

The letter that follows may prove interesting to the reader, as indicating a gracious willingness on the part of God to use very humble agency in saving souls; and also, as furnishing some evidence, that the death of Davis is one of the countless instrumentalities, by which Jesus will gather His people to Himself:

"NEW YORK. June 7, 1858.

" REVEREND AND DEAR SIR:

"IT is now little less than a year, since the occurrence of the painful and fatal accident to our mutual young friend, Davis Johnson.

" Scarcely a day has passed since that event, that he has not been brought to mind; sometimes by the course of circumstances in business, and sometimes involuntarily. His thorough and happy experience, and his final and glorious triumph in Christ, were scenes never to be forgotten. Even now his dying injunction rings in my ears: 'Tell them to be careful, very careful, for they know not what a day nor an hour may bring forth.'

" You doubtless have wondered that you have neither seen nor heard from me, since we parted at his grave; but, sir, though I have been pressed with the cares of business, almost incessantly, the whole year (which must be my apology for this seeming neglect), yet it has been pleasant to me to recall to mind often, your kind and earnest efforts for the salvation of my loved young friend.

"It will be gratifying to you to know, that the lesson taught by that dispensation of God, aided by your prayers, and that well directed and impressive circular, has done good work amongst the young gentlemen in our company; * * * * * * * * and I am happy to add that several of them are inquiring the way to Christ.

"I contemplate the pleasure of soon calling upon you.

"Respectfully, your friend and obedient servant, CHARLES DENNIS.

"REV. J. D. WELLS, Brooklyn, E. D."

This letter is published with the approval of the author, who wishes, with me, to throw all the light that God has been pleased to give, upon the dispensation of His providence, to which it refers.

And now, with this same end in view, I close the present chapter by directing attention to an important and interesting fact.

During all the earlier years of his life, and nearly to its close, Davis was under the influence of the truths as taught in the standards, and from the pulpits of the Reformed Protestant Dutch Church.

About a fortnight before his death, he was powerfully arrested, and made to think of death and eternity, under the ministry of a servant of Christ, connected with the Baptist Church. But it should be noticed, that in this first awakening, he was deeply conscious of the influence of early instruction and associations.

A week before his death, and after God had broken him in pieces, making him

"A wonder, tortured in the space
Betwixt this world, and that of grace,"

he was brought under the personal influence, and instruction, chiefly of two ministers of Christian denominations, differing from each other, and also from those mentioned before; the one a Methodist, and the other a Presbyterian.

Jesus said : "He that reapeth receiveth wages and gathereth fruit unto life eternal; that both he that soweth, and he that reapeth, may rejoice together." And Paul said, speaking by the Holy Ghost, "So then neither is he that planteth anything, neither he that watereth; but God that giveth the increase." And in the discovery and love of these sweet truths, Christians of every name must rejoice more and more, as they are made conscious of their oneness in Christ, and of their joint agency in the salvation of men, under Christ their Head.

CHAPTER XV.

Childhood.

"THE CHILDREN OF THY SERVANTS SHALL CONTINUE, AND THEIR SEED SHALL BE ESTABLISHED BEFORE THEE."

THE HOLY GHOST.

"Sow, in the morn, thy seed,
　　At eve, hold not thy hand;
　To doubt and fear give thou no heed,
　　Broad-cast it round the land.

"Thou canst not toil in vain;
　　Cold, heat, and moist, and dry,
　Shall foster and mature the grain,
　　For garners in the sky."

XV.

It is no part of my plan to write a biography of Davis. Of the last week only in his short life, I thought it my duty to speak particularly. But some readers may wish to know a little about his childhood. For these I add a few paragraphs, in a closing chapter.

He was the fifth son of Davis and Catharine Johnson, well known as residents of Williamsburgh, for many years. Here Davis was born, September 10th, 1837.

Love, filial and fraternal, was one of the earliest and sweetest signs of promise in his nature. When he came to his mother's feet, on Monday night, July 13th 1857, and putting his head into her lap, told her the new thoughts of his soul; and when, on Friday night, July 24th—the last night of his life—he repeatedly folded her to his heart, forgetting his pangs in her presence, he was constrained by a love that had grown with his growth, from the tenderest years of his childhood.

The same may be said of the love that prompted his visit to Williamsburgh on Saturday, the 18th of July, and also the arrangements for my second interview with him on Tuesday, the 21st of July. He was yearning ever a brother, whom he had loved from the first, and loved to the last, with a beautiful and a reciprocated love.

We have seen him maintaining the kind and thoughtful consideration of a gentleman, through all the days of his last week. This was because he had grown from childhood, into the habit of showing a proper regard for his obligations to others. On being re-proved, at the age of three and a half years, for saying at the table, "I want some bread," he instantly added, "Oh, I quite forgot, I'll thank you for some bread."

He was truthful from a child; and hence the testimony already given by his friend, who took him, when wearing a round-about, into the service of the Atlantic Mutual Insurance Company, and loved him to the end, "I could always rely on his word." His truthfulness, as one who knew him thoroughly, suggested, was not, perhaps, so much due to his fear of God, as to his pride. He was too proud to lie; he thought it unmanly and cowardly, as it is certainly most wicked.

And this suggests his independence of character. He was high-spirited and chiv-alrous, and not disposed to lean upon others. At a very early age, after entering on a business life, he insisted upon meeting his own expenses. And quite in keeping with this, he set his eye upon a mark far above any to which he was supposed to be looking, and pursued it steadily, and with great energy and success.

When he was eight years old, he went by permission and in company with an older brother, to bathe in the East River. Owing to some untoward circumstance, he lost his self-control, and sunk beneath the water. A gentleman, looking from a window at the instant, sprang through it, and pushing a boat from the shore, reached him, just as he was sinking the third time. And thus, in another way, the early youth of Davis, was a prophecy of later years. He received his "mortal hurt" in the same waters, and not far from the same spot.

And one thing more. As he lay sick, from his exposure in the water on the occa-

sion referred to, he received from the venerable, and still living superintendent of the
Sabbath School, to which he belonged, a
Bible, as a reward for the recitation of
many verses of the Scriptures. The precious seed of that early sowing did not
mature, till he lay broken and dying, from
his second exposure to the "perils of
waters."

And now the harvest for him has ended.
The fruits of righteousness, brought to per-
fection in his nature under the heavenly
culture, are all garnered.

The work was God's, and the glory shall
be His.

"And I heard a voice from heaven, saying unto me : Write. Blessed are the dead
that die in the Lord from henceforth. Yea,
saith the Spirit, that they may rest from
their labours, and their works do follow
them."

www.ingramcontent.com/pod-product-compliance
Lightning Source LLC
Chambersburg PA
CBHW030548040726
47497CB00008B/2625